CW00956274

Advice *from* Angels

Messages from the angels we meet every day

CHRISSIE ASTELL

Dedicated to my own angels, Daniel
and Claire, with love.

First published in Great Britain in 2005 by
Godsfield Press, a division of Octopus Publishing Group Ltd

This edition published in 2011 by Bounty Books,
a division of Octopus Publishing Group Ltd,
Endeavour House, 189 Shaftesbury Avenue, London WC2H 8JY
www.octopusbooks.co.uk

An Hachette UK Company
www.hachette.co.uk

Printed and bound in China

ISBN 978-0-753721-49-0

Advice *from* Angels

Contents

INTRODUCTION

Angels are beings of light. Messengers of God, angels are intermediaries between humankind and the Divine. Healers, protectors, bearers of information and joy, sources of inspiration, guardians and friends, they come to us in many ways and give advice and counsel that is both practical and uplifting. Angels don't have to prove themselves. They just are.

Whoever you are, whatever your faith, and whether or not you believe these words, you have been given a wonderful gift – the love of angels. This gift has been given freely, and you can choose to accept or refuse. Having accepted it with gratitude, you are asked to share it with others at every opportunity. All faiths instruct us to love one another. This teaching is not just a sugary sentiment; it asks you to act truly from the heart as angels do.

Angels in vast numbers are sent to Earth to help us in our humanness and assist our spiritual growth. Many people have already awakened to their call for realignment, attunement and enlightenment. When you tune in to the wonderful energy of angels, you are instantly aware of the love that emanates from their presence – a love that ignites a spark in the heart that can never be extinguished.

Never be misled by the use of the word love. There is no implication of 'softness' here. Being kind in action and thoughtful in a loving way does not make you a doormat. Angels are not soft and feathery. Appointed as our guides, guardians and protectors of justice, angels are the soldiers of Heaven!

Archangel Michael, Lord of the Archangels, is portrayed armed with a sword and bears God's holy armour. His role is to protect, and he is often shown slaying the dragon. A spiritual warrior and defender of right, he inspires us to cut away the dross in our own lives and defend our truth as we venture along life's journey.

We can all act with power but in a loving manner. It is mothering without smothering, being of service without the need to control or dominate. Acting with love is acting as the angels would. If we all behaved like angels, Earth would be a lot more like Heaven!

By inviting the angels into our lives and receiving their guidance, we ignite the Divine spark within us – that part of us that is linked to the angels. Imagine the enthusiasm generated when we light that spark and they see it glowing and growing. All we need is pureness of intention and a loving heart.

Whether or not you already work closely with the angelic forces, you will feel the energy of their love in this beautiful little book. Allow yourself to be inspired by the joy captured in these words of angelic wisdom. Allow the spark of angelic love to be kindled in your heart and make your world a little more Heavenly.

This book will inspire your thoughts, nourish your being, warm your heart and ignite the angelic spark within you. It will lovingly remind you that you are never alone because there is always an angel by your side.

Angel-being

'Utopia will come to pass only when we grow wings and all people are converted to angels.'

FEDOR DOSTOEVSKY

The celestial beings are only one of the many aspects of Divine essence. God is everywhere. As human beings we are made up of the four elements – air, water, earth and fire – but we are powered by the energy of the Divine within. How can we believe that we are separate from God in any way? When there is joy in the world we celebrate as one. How can we not know that, when one suffers, the whole consciousness of the Earth takes part in that pain?

When we pollute the rivers, when we cut down the trees, when we hunt down animals until they are extinct, can we not feel the universal sorrow? You have the capacity for great healing and joy. The creativity and love of the angels combined with the ingenuity of human intellect can blend to a fine force. Recognize that power within you and dedicate it to the whole. You will be amazed at the gifts that power will give you.

'I have been on the verge of being an angel all my life, but it has never happened yet.'

MARK TWAIN

When you start to work with the angels you won't suddenly become a different person. You won't become unrecognizable, looking ten years younger or twenty pounds lighter, and all your worries will not miraculously fade away. You will have the same personality traits and probably the same aches and pains too! Inviting the angels into your life is not meant to improve you or make you a better person. It simply allows you to connect with your real self, and reminds you who you really are. It will enable you to open your heart, connect with your soul, your higher self, your intuition and your companion angels.

Working with angels is not fluffy, happy-clappy, feel-good stuff. Far from it! You will become stronger, more focused, confident, compassionate, self-reliant, connected, centred and authentic. The changes are not necessarily physical … or are they?

Don't worry if you fall on your face while learning to fly – practice makes perfect.

This is a time of consciousness raising, but also a time of consciousness crushing. We live in a time when spirituality is acknowledged as an essential part of life, and yet a life of spirituality is ignored or ridiculed.

So what do you do when you have found your path of spiritual truth and you want to follow it? Honour yourself, and practise. Practise by example, using humour, serenity, humility, kindness and sincerity. You will be helped in your challenge, with your choices, and with directions. The angels will work through synchronicity to send into your life the circumstances and people you need to support you. You can do this; you can fly.

'The more we love what is good and true, the more the angels love to be with us.'

EMANUEL SWEDENBORG

The gift of life contains no promises, only possibilities. We are called to live our lives with appropriate regard for others. We are interdependent with all things on our wonderful planet. If you sincerely immerse yourself in the service of others you cannot help but be helped yourself. Rather than ask what you can get from life, ask: 'How may I serve? What can I contribute?' Many blessings are around you everywhere, so don't miss the opportunity to make a difference.

We are all angels – it's what we do with our wings that makes us different.

There was a forest fire and all the animals were fleeing for their lives, except for one little humming bird who was busy flying among the high-growing blossoms.

As a monkey went swinging by in the tops of the trees he called to the humming bird: 'Come on, you're going to burn, we all have to fly for our lives.' 'No, I can't,' said the little humming bird as she visited another flower, filled her tiny beak with nectar, flew back and poured the drop of moisture on to the flames. She flew to the next flower to repeat the process. 'No, no, you must hurry,' chattered the monkey nervously. 'You'll die if you don't come now.' 'Not at the moment,' said the little humming bird, flying quickly to another blossom and filling her beak with nectar. 'But what are you doing?' asked the monkey impatiently. 'I am doing my bit,' said the humming bird finally.

You don't have to be a great enlightened master or an expert to be able to do your bit. It is how you do it that is more important; it is your *intention* to serve the greater purpose that counts.

God wants spiritual fruits not religious nuts!

Fanaticism and dogma are not enlightening. Is it not better to gently sow the seeds of wisdom and love into areas of strife, allowing them to grow in their own time? You are on your own spiritual journey, and are always in the right place at the right time, even though the decisions you make may affect your progress at times. Don't be afraid that someone else may seem 'more spiritual' than you. Your light is just as bright; don't be afraid to let it shine.

There is nothing 'spiritual' or enlightening about imposing one's intellectual truth on someone else. All the great masters taught in simple parables and stories that made their teachings accessible to all levels of understanding. How motivating and inspiring it can be to share ideas with like-minded people who are now harvesting the fruits of their own spiritual maturity.

'A good tree cannot bear bad fruit, a bad tree cannot bear good fruit ... by their fruits you will know them.'

MATTHEW 7

The kind words of an angel may brighten the hour and lighten the day.

'I want you to know,' said the stranger, 'that you have helped me through my depression and my life is back on track, thanks to you.' 'Sorry, I don't know what you mean,' replied the young woman, wishing she had not answered the door.

'Well, every time I saw you walking down the street, you gave me a warm smile and passed the time of day with me. When you drove past in your car, you waved as if you knew me. Your smile brightened my day and lifted me somehow. You made me feel as if someone really cared. I just thought I'd find out where you lived so that I could tell you how grateful I am. It wasn't hard to find you. I just asked if anyone knew the young woman with an old "Beetle" car and a smile like an angel.' A few kind words cost nothing but the effort.

Once you open and stretch your wings, you'll see feathers everywhere.

Open your wings and be the angel that you can be. Sit, your eyes closed, breathe deeply and relax; let go any stresses and anxieties held in your body. Visualize your guardian angel behind you with open hands poised over your shoulders. Imagine the warmth of loving energy coming from those healing hands.

Visualize your angel placing an index finger on each of your vertebrae, down your spine. Imagine you have two unused folded wings attached to your shoulder blades. Ask your angel to open your wings. Feel their wonderful strength and softness. The angel encases them in a divine radiance visible to all angels of light. In gratitude, breathing deeply, bring yourself back into the moment. Hold the sensation of becoming an angel and feel empowered to share love and joy in every situation.

Guide and guard your thoughts, and give the angels a chance to guide and guard you.

If we dwell on negativity by judging others, or being overly self-critical, how can the angels possibly 'get in' to give us the guidance we ask for?

Try this exercise. First imagine your favourite person, the one you hold most dear. Hold on to that feeling of love. Now in your imagination go to your favourite place. Bring to mind the sheer joy of it and smile. Now attach those two feelings, first love then joy. How do you feel? Blissful, isn't it? Get right into the feeling and give it a name such as 'angel-bliss' or a colour like rose-pink.

For the rest of the day try to be aware of how many times you hold on to negative thoughts. Each time you think critically of yourself or another, stop and be aware of your body. Does it feel relaxed or tense? Having observed yourself, immediately let go of the negative thought without judgement and think 'angel-bliss' and surround yourself in your chosen colour.

'If we were all a little more like angels, the Earth would be a little more like Heaven.'

KAREN GOLDMAN

When someone does a kind deed unexpectedly or turns up when most needed, we often say 'Oh, you are an angel!' Imagine what a wonderful place this would be if we automatically treated one another as the angels do, with unconditional kindness and love. Everyday disagreements would be dealt with gently and with care for one another's feelings. There would be no need for wars, as no one would need to control another.

Close your eyes for a moment and breathe the wonderful sensation of love, joy, harmony and peace. As you breathe out, imagine that with every exhalation you are filling a bubble with these feelings. As the bubble of joy expands to enormous size, visualize it floating upwards into the stars and bursting, showering sparkling fragments of angelic peace everywhere on Earth.

Your angels are not there to judge you, only love you.

Acting with love is acting with discernment but not judgement. How easy it is to judge others and ourselves harshly. Society needs public laws to protect the vulnerable and maintain safety and justice. But in spiritual life it is better to simply observe selfish behaviour without casting judgement. Then we are able to teach by example by maintaining our own inner peace. We are not condoning the misdemeanour, but we can refrain from being judgemental.

To observe without judgement, call on Archangel Zadkiel and the Violet Ray. Visualize a vivid violet light permeating your mind. Ask God and the angels to purify and transmute the negative feelings into compassion, wisdom and love and how best to deal with the situation. Thank Zadkiel and use this technique whenever you are faced with a negative situation.

The art of an angel is the heart of an angel.

How good are you at sharing with others? Most of us share friendship and fun together but how easy is it to share our private feelings? Our thoughts, ideas and love, the reality of who we really are, these are often kept very close to our hearts for fear of rejection, ridicule, criticism and pain.

Sharing is a two-way living experience. The universal law of generosity works in such a way that what you give willingly will be returned to you, sometimes more fully.

Sit meditatively and create a safe space for yourself, then call upon the Angels of Harmony to draw close to you. Ask the angels to help dissolve any barriers of poverty-consciousness or rejection that prevent you from sharing either your material possessions or your feelings. Surround yourself in a pink loving light of warmth and know that you are always supported in your generosity.

'Angels can fly because they take themselves lightly.'

G.K. CHESTERTON

As incarnate beings we need gravity for stability and to stay grounded. But the word gravity also means laden, serious, solemnity, sobriety and importance. Heavy indeed! Perhaps as human beings dependent on gravity we take ourselves too seriously and become a little self-important. Certainly, in some dogmatic religious teachings, the spiritual path is laden with *gravitas*.

The angels are also charged with the heavier aspects of spiritual life such as responsibility, courage, efficiency, dedication, truth, justice, commitment and education. But they carry their responsibilities with joy, freedom, abundance, celebration, synchronicity, wonder, openness and love. Most of all they perform their tasks with a lightness that comes from complete trust in Divine wisdom.

Make a set of 'angel cards', one with each attribute, remembering that the more serious ones are to give you strength in a positive way. Choose one each day, thanking the angel of whichever quality you have chosen. Celebrate your choice by affirming that quality as your own.

'Be not forgetful to entertain strangers, for in so doing some have entertained angels unawares.'

HEBREWS 13:2

Jo had been repelled by a tramp at the door asking for food. Wishing to be charitable, she brought him sandwiches and a drink. There was something unnerving about the man's stare. His eyes were blue and piercing, yet gentle and 'all-knowing'. Spreading a rag on the grass he sat to eat and thanked her for her kindness. After a few minutes he had gone leaving no sign, but a beautiful white feather floated on to the kitchen table.

Angelic Guidance

'Any sort of pretence seems unworthy of angels.'

SAINT THOMAS AQUINAS

Often the decisions we make create self-imposed challenges, which are wonderful opportunities for spiritual growth. But, if we do not face the challenge, not only will we miss a chance to move on, we will have to face the same challenge over and over until we do confront it.

Be honest with yourself. If you deceive yourself by pretending that everything is perfect your goals become hazy, you bury your potential brilliance under layers of self-deception and illusion and you defeat your quest for self-improvement. Ask the angels for help!

Archangel Michael,
using your sword of justice help me to cut away
the parts of my life that are shrouded with deception.
Help me to see only that which is honest and true.
Stay by my side and give me the strength to face each situation
with courage and absolute honesty, knowing that I am
supported and lovingly guided forward into the light.

'The beauty in an angel's face lies not in its form but in the feeling it leaves with you.'

BRAHMA KUMARIS

Appearances can be deceptive. Not all strangers are angels and some beauty is only skin-deep. 'Beware of false prophets who come to you in sheep's clothing, but inwardly are ravenous wolves' (Matthew 7). There are thousands of spiritual teachers, gurus and facilitators; not all will be suited to you. Before you choose, develop your intuition and discernment.

Meditate on this by imagining a circle of golden light, with you and the Angel of Discernment standing in the centre. Visualize all the people currently of importance in your life standing outside the circle. One by one invite them to enter and walk past you and the Angel of Discernment. Your angel will allow only those who are beneficial to your spiritual growth to remain in the circle; all others she will ask to pass on. Simply observe, do not allow your mind to judge at this stage. Listen to your body and your reactions. Learn to trust that the angels are guiding your feelings.

'If you want to tell anything to God, tell it to the wind.'

AFRICAN PROVERB

Listen to your inner being. Only in the stillness of the depths of the soul can you know God. Find the small voice within. Everything you experience is remembered. Every answer is found within. Only in the silence can the answers be heard. But sometimes this is forgotten and so we pray out loud to articulate our fear or despair, or to plead for guidance.

When you speak out you affirm your thoughts to the Universe. You sense them through hearing the words as well as thinking and feeling them. If you talk to your angels, the messages are carried directly to God. If you pray directly to God the angels respond immediately. Voice your prayers out loud to the Universe, choose your words carefully, open your heart ... the angels are there.

'Outside the doors of study. . .
an angel awaits.'

HANNAH GREEN

Sometimes, in striving to do our best, we become so obsessed with work or study that we forget we are spiritual beings in human form. Our journey is to bring knowledge gained into our spiritual life and our spirituality into everyday life. We become so wrapped up in our personal agenda that we often forget that life is not meant to be difficult. Challenging, perhaps, but smoother than most of us realize. Ask Archangel Gabriel and God's Angels of Wisdom to guide you with love back on to your spiritual path.

'The Earth is to the sun what mankind is to the angels.'

VICTOR HUGO

Without the sun the Earth would perish in cold darkness. Imagine the Earth without sunlight, without heat, without sunrise and sunset. Nothing would live. Humanity could not survive without light, but what of spiritual light? How do we illuminate the soul?

Archangel Jophiel and the Angels of Illumination are there to turn the light on in your heart and enlighten your spiritual pathway. In all aspects of creativity you can call for Jophiel's assistance.

Begin by lighting a candle and sitting quietly. Now imagine you are surrounded by an infusion of clear golden-yellow light glowing around you. Call to Archangel Jophiel and the Angels of Illumination and visualize them encircling you with their loving light energy. As you breathe in, flood your whole body with this light. Imagine yourself drawing in clarity, creativity and inspiration. With every out-breath see density, confusion, darkness and discouragement dissolved by the angels' golden light.

When an angel points the way, you'll see the light at the end of the tunnel.

We know that angels can appear in many guises. I have so often asked for guidance from the angels and then opened a book or heard a conversation that gave me the very insight I needed. Sometimes we struggle on our own, believing that our strength is in our independence and that we must do it alone. God doesn't need us to struggle on blindly. Our growth comes with the realization that we are NOT alone. Ask for help when you feel ready.

Archangel Raphael, I am now ready to heal;
place your loving hand upon my heart and cleanse
and purify anything there that is not of your kind.
Place your hand upon my head and cleanse
and purify my thoughts, enabling me to think and
know only what is true.
Place your finger upon my brow to help me open my
third eye to your wisdom, so that I may intuitively discern
what is right. Thank you.

Don't be afraid of the dark, it is only the light casting shadows.

It has been said that the brighter we shine, the more shadow we create. Sometimes these are the shadows within ourselves, those darker areas that we may not want to know about. Becoming spiritually aware means facing those inner demons, confronting them with gratitude, dealing with them and moving on. If we really wish to commit to change, then we have help readily available.

Sit quietly and, as you relax with your eyes closed, breathe deeply and let go of any tension in your body with each exhalation. Invite your angel to stand by your side. Imagine a blank screen in front of you. Ask the angel to show you aspects of yourself that need work and watch the screen. You may see a full image rather like a dream, or simple objects; you may hear music or words or experience a feeling.

What seems like death to a caterpillar is the birth of a beautiful butterfly to the Master.

What a fantasy – to feast to our heart's content, wrap ourselves in a warm cocoon, fall into a deep sleep and wake up to find ourselves transformed into a being of delicate beauty with wings to fly wherever we choose.

Nothing is really that simple. Firstly, the earthbound caterpillar is driven by need, insatiable hunger. It is not free until it has changed from this caterpillar phase. If we are prepared to completely change from our insatiable 'needs' we are all capable of metamorphosizing into beautiful beings of light.

It is through really letting go of your old self, and dying metaphorically, that the new you can come truly into the light. This is what the Master Jesus meant when he said we must all be born again.

Sometimes the angel's gift is not to give you what you want.

To want is an expression of need. It tells the Universe that there is a lack, a void, a wanting within us. Remember the old adage given to demanding children: 'I want never gets'? Imagine constantly telling the Universe 'I want more' – in other words, negatively affirming that you are living in a permanent state of lack! Better to create affirmations that reinforce what is already yours.

Instead of saying 'I want to be slimmer' or 'I wish I felt good', say 'My body grows more youthful every day and all my cells work in perfect harmony'.

Instead of saying 'I can't afford so-and-so', say 'I live in abundance, I always have enough'. Notice the difference when you change 'I want someone to love me' to 'I am lovable and I attract loving people in my life'.

Share your secret dreams with the angels and watch as they all come true.

It is said that the angels already know the higher plan for our lives. They sense our hopes and dreams, but cannot interfere with our human choices. This would be interfering with the laws of karma. We are given circumstances where choices can be made, but as humans we often make this difficult for ourselves.

When petitioning the angels remember that intention and interpretation are important. Angels are not like a 'genie of the lamp'; they don't fulfil your every desire. But wherever possible, and if your wish is for the highest possible good of all concerned, it is likely that you will have a favourable outcome.

Angels respect your right to be human.

We are all part of this fascinating creation. We are all unique, special and loved. It would be foolish to think of ourselves as perfect, however, since that would create an almost impossible position for us to have to live up to.

Marianne Williamson says: 'we are born to make manifest the glory of God that is within us. It is not in some of us; it is in everyone.' We have chosen to become human beings, to incarnate with a role to play. The angels are here to help us achieve our goals. With prayer, meditation and an honest desire we can do the right thing, most of the time.

And when we don't? We are truly loved unconditionally, which means all the time, regardless of poor choices and our human frailties. As we liberate ourselves from the fear of failure, our confidence and trust carry us forward and our presence automatically liberates others.

'The beautiful souls are they that are universal, open and are ready for all things.'

MICHEL DE MONTAIGNE

Laughter and fun are gifts to us. Many things are serious and saddening, and many challenges are unimaginably difficult. Learning to laugh at oneself and release the 'ego' part of ourselves that wants to be taken seriously has an amazing effect. If we lose ego and accept that we are small and childlike in relation to the Universe we can begin to lighten up and fly. We can have fun and see enjoyment in everything we do while at the same time dedicating the right amount of responsibility required by the task. We are born to be free.

The only chains we place on ourselves are unnecessary burdens of guilt, domination and pride. Once we let go of these chains, and let go of the need to dominate or control others we become lighter, happier, freer and able to feel the spring in our step and the air in our wings! Unburden yourself by trying the following visualization.

Sit quietly and imagine all your burdens and responsibilities as weighted belts around your wrists, ankles and waist. Call Archangel Michael and your guardian angels closer to you and visualize unfastening

your weighty belts. Hand them to your angels. Imagine that the angels exchange each weight with a beautiful bright balloon. As you give each weight away allow yourself to feel lighter physically. Now ask Archangel Michael to cut the strings of the balloons representing the burdens that have already been relieved and watch as they fly into the sky, carrying your cares away, leaving you light and free to fly like the angel that you are.

'Some people really see angels where others see an empty space.'

John Ruskin

There are a few guidelines when you start to tune in to your angels and want to see them. Don't try too hard; just allow the vision to appear. Be prepared to be surprised. Try not to hold on to preconceived ideas of what you will see or hope to see.

Some people see sparkling lights; others smell a wonderful fragrance, yet see nothing. Many see a bright light and occasionally an outline of a form. Thousands of people have experienced angelic encounters of help or reassurances by a stranger, who then disappears, particularly in hospitals or during accidents.

It is more common to see nothing yet be aware of a calming, loving presence. Allow yourself to believe. Your prayers will be answered.

'The angel's intelligence is alight with the penetrating simplicity of divine concepts.'

DIONYSIUS

It is not surprising that our lives are full of confusion. By piling on the pressure, we create an existence of turmoil and disharmony. Sit back for a moment and consider which of today's tasks are truly essential. If you do not complete them all will the moon refuse to shine? It is the ego that insists on cramming all this non-essential clutter into our lives – the fear of failure, the fear of rejection. There is an easier way.

Give this day's tasks over in your mind to the angels and to God. Ask for the clarity of purpose of the Divine plan for your life. Ask that all your decisions and actions today are for the greater good of your higher consciousness, and for the highest good of all concerned.

As you clarify your actions and prioritize your day to the highest purpose, the angels will have the opportunity to guide and assist. Keep it simple, concentrate your Divine light and watch your plan unfold.

An angel is like a sanctuary where the door is always open and you can sit and feel the peace.

You know the feeling when you wish the world would go away and leave you alone, when the future looks bleak and your mind is full of confusion and doubt. Most of us have been there. But there are ways to get through these times. In the midst of your grey feelings, try this uplifting exercise.

Light a candle to signify the light. Whenever a candle is lit the angels draw closer. In the light of the candle bring to mind ten things for which you are grateful. Start with the simplest things like the air you breathe, the ground you walk on, the sun, the sky, the moonlight and stars. Add ten more, perhaps people or places you love, and then another ten. Before you realize you will have a never-ending list.

Invite your angel to share these thoughts with you and ask that you be free to find your way back into the light in your own time, in the loving peace of your angel's sanctuary.

Angel Reassurance

'An angel is like a mirror that reflects the truth kindly, for in its reflection you can see who you truly are.'

ANTHEA CHURCH

Have you noticed how many different masks you wear? By developing a mask for every occasion you are pretending to be someone else. Have you forgotten who you really are? You dilute your own energies, your personal magnetism and diminish your potential for growth by ignoring your true self. Be courageous. Acknowledge your true self every day. Affirm your ability to be true to yourself. Call on your guardian angel and ask to be given the courage and honesty to be who you truly are.

'The thoughts and actions of angels are not limited by time and space.'

EMANUEL SWEDENBORG

Angels are not tied to our three-dimensional reality. They have no concept of time and space, moving freely and instantly between our world and theirs. An angel's movement is as quick as a thought. The great archangels can be in several places at any given time. Don't be afraid that your personal dilemma is too insignificant to lay before an archangel, or that you will not be heard.

There are major catastrophes in the world and these need great shifts of understanding and human intervention. These are overseen by archangels at every given moment, but so are you. The archangels can do both. The energetic loving energy they emit is beyond our human understanding.

A true request, for the right reasons, is never too simple nor too small to be heard by the angels. You are loved and important. Never forget that.

To follow in an angel's footsteps, tread lightly.

When we come to a point in our spiritual growth where we feel we have made a discovery, it is easy to become overly enthusiastic and thrust our new-found information on anyone who will listen. How often do we give unsolicited advice?

However, there are spiritual laws that we need to understand. We must take responsibility for our own spiritual growth and release others to do the same. Loving or sharing through force of will without compassion can be seen as a form of violence. Gently and lovingly honour your truth whilst honouring the right of others to theirs.

Angels do not interfere in our lives; they allow us to make our own choices, to grow at our own pace. Our own commitment to spiritual growth, in love, is the only measure of our progress – not how well we compare with others.

Angels are there to nourish our being, not to feed our egos.

A hundred years ago almost everyone believed in God in one form or another. Every nation had a form of religious belief that was part of its culture. Now most countries are known politically as secular societies. Yet human beings require nurturing of mind, body and spirit. People are hungry to fulfil a yearning to be complete.

The angels can help us. Truly ecumenical, angels act as a link between God and us, as messengers, conveying our thoughts and prayers to the source. On the returning impulse of loving energy they prompt and guide us in our thoughts and dreams. This enables our spiritual growth through love so that we begin to understand how precious we truly are.

An angel may save the day and sometimes your whole life.

Annie was in a devastating relationship. She desperately needed to leave with her children and start afresh. As she sat at the bus stop a stranger sat down next to her and told her that she would find the courage she needed to change her life. The stranger then got up and walked away, without waiting for the bus to arrive.

Feeling puzzled by the potency of the stranger's words, Annie felt inspired, reassured and motivated. She packed and left for safety that weekend, and never looked back.

Remember that, when you ask angels for help, silence is sometimes the best answer.

Like children constantly needing reassurance and support, it is very tempting to ask the angels for help with absolutely everything. We may trust that we are Divinely guided, but should also trust that we have a huge amount of wisdom and knowledge within. Whether referred to as an 'inner knowing' or 'higher self', our own resources are largely untapped.

We have the ability to use our intuition and, as we develop spiritually, our inner knowing/higher self becomes easier to access. We have an immeasurable capacity within for self-healing, making choices and 'knowing' the answers. Universal law will not allow the angels to interfere in our life plan.

Sit silently with each decision, ask the angels for guidance and hold the silence, connecting with your own deep sense of 'knowing'. By learning to read the 'signs' all around, you will soon be shown if you are going in the right direction.

Only fear stops you from flying, so spread your wings and enjoy the rush!

What prevents us from reaching the top of the ladder? What stops us from allowing ourselves to go with the flow, fly with the breeze?

The answer is our fear of failure. Yet the message of the angels is clear: there is no such thing as failure. Each time we try to fly, successfully or not, we learn and grow.

Believe in yourself as the angels do. Believe in your ability to know instinctively that whatever you are doing with honest intention is always right. Go ahead and trust yourself. True happiness is allowing yourself to be who you really are.

'Come to the edge!' Life said
'We are afraid' They said
'Come to the edge!' Life said
They came
It pushed them
and they flew …

GUILLAUME APPOLLINAIRE 1880–1918

Angels are always there, even when you think the rest of the world has gone away.

We are never alone. When we feel sad, lonely and even unloved, we need to remember that each of us has a guardian angel who knows and loves us even though no one else seems to care. In a quiet peaceful place it is possible to think things through with your guardian angel who already knows all your problems and secrets. Talk out loud to your angels and ask for a sign that is meaningful to you.

Practise listening and feeling as a form of meditation; this will bring the presence of the angels closer to you until a sense of 'knowing' is developed as a form of communication between you and your angels. Feathers are a Divine symbol that your angels are with you.

An angel can touch you without being physical.

Angels can speak to you in the form of visions, dreams, whispers, nudges, feelings or a sense of knowing. Many people are 'clairaudient' and can hear words spoken to them. Some are 'clairvoyant' and can see things which others cannot see. Others are 'clairsentient' and feel a presence. Each of these is a gift that can be developed and used for the benefit of others. The most common feelings described by people are 'goose-bumps', a tingling of the scalp or feeling that their hair is being touched. Sometimes there is a change of temperature and a sense of 'music' or a fragrance of flowers, particularly roses.

You don't have to see an angel in its physical form to know that you have been encouraged or helped; you will feel it in your inner being. Allow yourself to believe in your heart. You will know for yourself. You do not need to prove it to anybody else.

'Angels may not always come when you call them, but they will come when you need them.'

KAREN GOLDMAN

Like demanding children we can ask too much of the angels, and develop a sense of lazy expectancy, relying on someone else to do things for us. Listen to your inner being. Find the still small voice within. Everything we have ever experienced we remember deep in our bodies; our memory is not just in the brain, but also in our very cells. We are capable of helping ourselves because we often do know the answers.

It is important not to trivialize the angelic realms by becoming dependent and petitioning angels for help with every little thing in life. When you are truly in need, when your heart and soul seek ardently, you will find angels lovingly by your side showing you the way.

Once an angel has touched you, you will never be the same again.

Are angels imaginary? The imagination is the creative expression of everything we know. Every experience is stored away in our soul memory. Certain thoughts, dreams or words can stimulate the creative aspect in our memory that triggers a vision in our mind's eye.

Angels present themselves in a manner that is acceptable to each individual. When you hear an angel speak to you, or feel the loving wisdom touch your heart, when you stand in the presence of your guardian angel, whether in your dreams or physical reality, not only will you never forget, but your life will never be the same again.

'For an angel a minute can be a thousand years, for time to angels is measured in love.'

Anthea Church

Have you lived your life rather like the White Rabbit in *Alice's Adventures in Wonderland*, dashing here and there with a pocket-watch in your hand fretting about being late? This man-made phenomenon 'time' is a concept of little significance to the celestial realms. A moment of our time may as well be a thousand years.

If we are on a spiritual journey we may be amazed at the speed of our development or levels of learning. We start to fly with the angels. But, to our disappointment, we slide back into our normal routine for a while, feeling that perhaps we are forgotten. You cannot be in a 'peak experience' all the time. If you fly near the sun too often, you will soon burn your wings.

Your angels are still there; no more than a fleeting moment has passed in their terms. They never go away. Their patience is immeasurable; after all, they may have been waiting for you all your life!

Humans must be known to be loved, angels must be loved to be known.

When we love and are being loved our souls sing. We are nourished and whole. We cannot exist without love. Loving others is often easy, but in order to love completely and unconditionally we must first learn to love ourselves. Loving is an expression of kindness, of communicating from the heart and of compassion. Learn to give the gift of love to yourself.

Think of a quality you deeply admire, one you would attribute to an angel. Visualize that quality in the form of a flower bud and in your imagination carry it deep within yourself, to your very core. Now look at the flower and admire it, appreciate its beauty, its perfume and its perfection. Remembering those qualities, recognize that you, too, have these attributes. Acknowledge and respect yourself for that.

Recognizing that your soul is a spark of the Divine and that it contains perfection like that of the flower, allow yourself to love your soul. Your soul has the qualities of an angel. As you begin to know that part of yourself, you will learn how to love yourself.

'Angels are like perfect guests – they always bring gifts and are never a burden.'

Anthea Church

Many of the gifts given to us by angels are in the form of dreams and visions. Take yourself into a meditative state by sitting comfortably while listening to some gentle music. Visualize walking on a mountainside with a marvellous view all around. Imagine that you are walking higher where the air is pure and fragrant. Ahead of you is a beautiful golden gate. As you walk towards it, the gate opens slowly and you are surrounded by amazingly bright golden light. Breathe in the light, allowing it to enfold and infuse you.

Now imagine that you stand before your guardian angel, the most beautiful being you have ever dreamed of. The angel greets you, embraces you and gives you a special gift. Stand in the light of the angel, bathing in love and acceptance. With gratitude in your heart, knowing that you may return at any time, leave the angel when you are ready.

Walk down the mountain; at the bottom take a few deep breaths and bring your awareness into your feet, hands and face. Being fully present in the here and now, reflect on your gift and how you can use it.

Angels in Action

Friends are angels who lift our feet when our own wings have forgotten how to fly.

A young child was brought into the hospital on a stretcher. She was unconscious and accompanied by her parents and a policeman. Lucy had run into the middle of a very busy road where a truck had hit her and run over her twice. She was examined and only a small bruise on her shoulder was found. Just before being sent for X-rays she opened her eyes and smiled. 'Where is the man in white?' she demanded. The doctor came forward. 'No, no, the man in the long white, shiny dress.' As her mother stroked her face, Lucy said, 'That man stroked my face as he picked up the wheels.'

When your light is shining at its brightest, beware of attracting too many moths.

When we open ourselves psychically we can become susceptible to interference from beings that are not necessarily useful to us. It is very important to learn how to protect yourself.

Primarily, call on Archangel Michael for protection and imagine an instant blue light surrounding you. Visualize a cloak of blue wrapped around you and request the protection of Archangel Michael's sword.

You can visualize yourself in a strong white light, like a spotlight, that is with you all the time. If you wish, circle yourself with a golden light and ask that it protect you with Universal love and light. Choose whichever method feels right for you and make a determined effort to establish it as one of your daily spiritual practices. At the same time ask for the gift of discernment, that the angels will guide you to only what is right and true for the highest possible good of all concerned.

Angels provide you with the ingredients to create your own miracles.

Karma is simply translated as 'cause and effect'. An angel cannot change karma. Once we become aware of the effectiveness of our own behaviour we can petition the angels for help in making better decisions for the best possible outcome.

Call on the specific qualities of the great archangels to help you:

- Archangel Michael protects from the influence of others.
- Archangel Gabriel will help with direction and sanctification.
- Archangel Uriel will help you to find inner peace.
- Archangel Jophiel will illuminate and enlighten you with Divine wisdom.
- Archangel Zadkiel can assist with transmuting negativity into positive energy and bring joy.
- Archangel Raphael will help you to heal at all levels.
- Archangel Chamuel will help you to overcome low self-esteem and bring unconditional love into your life.

You can see the love of angels reflected in the faces of sleeping children.

There is a theory that many children being born now are old souls with highly developed spiritual skills. These very special children will remind us of long-forgotten healing techniques, psychic awareness and immeasurable compassion.

A beautiful story came to me recently. A young mother became very worried by her five-year-old son's obsession with wanting to be left on his own with the new baby. She stood quietly outside the bedroom door and allowed him to put his little sister into her crib. Slightly fearful, she closed the door when he asked her to 'go away' but remained listening and ready to run into the bedroom. Tears rolled down her cheeks when, to her surprise, he kissed his little sister and said: 'Please help me to remember what it was like. I've forgotten already.'

An angel will never give up on you, even if you have given up on yourself!

Many of us are plagued by feelings of unworthiness or low self-esteem. Keep in mind that all thoughts create energy, and like attracts like. When we focus on negative thinking, we attract disappointments and disasters.

Archangel Chamuel and the Angels of Love can help you overcome negative feelings if you ask. Close your eyes and ask that angelic love surround you. Banish negative thinking by saying, three times, 'Be gone feelings of anti-love!' See yourself surrounded by bright pink light and feel instantly uplifted.

Remember, also, that your guardian angels are with you even when you are feeling negative. You are special to your angels no matter how you are feeling about yourself. Whenever you need reassurance, guidance, protection and love, just call on them for help. Soon you will be shown the way to happiness again.

Angels don't always blow their own trumpets – the noise would be deafening!

There is no need to list all the wonderful things that angels do. Similarly, there is no need to tell the world how wonderful you are when you do something wonderful for someone else. Spontaneous acts of kindness need no fanfare. The person receiving your generosity of spirit knows what you have done, as do the angels. Nothing is missed.

Archangel Metatron and the Recording Angels collect every thought and action in the Akashic Records – that cosmic storehouse of doers and deeds. When you do something wonderful, Metatron takes note. Yet keep in mind that the kindest acts are those we do without expecting recognition or reward.

Treat everyone you meet with love – they may be angels in disguise.

Angels and Ascended Masters are able to manifest in different forms. Very often the guise chosen is not what you would expect; remember that angels are non-denominational and the pictures we may have of blond, blue-eyed angels are our own imagination too.

I have heard of angels appearing as beggars, blind old men, little old ladies, tall Rastafarians, even angelic truck-drivers. Angels are always around to help us when we really need them, but do we always feel the same way? By treating everyone as you would like to be treated, by showing kindness at every opportunity, you too are spreading unconditional angelic love in action.

As you kindle the spark of angelic light within your heart, notice the glow in others.

Once you light the spark of Divinity in your own heart you will feel a joy that you may not have experienced before. Your attitude to life may change and the world may seem a much more beautiful place. As you act towards others with love and notice how they respond with warmth to you, you will attract more loving people around you.

Imagine a spark of golden light glowing in your heart. Close your eyes and visualize this loving angelic spark spreading its warmth and love through your chest. As you breathe deeply, imagine this warm glow filling your whole body, legs, feet, arms, hands and through your neck and throat into your head. Imagine that this wonderful loving light spreads out of your pores, glowing all over your skin.

Now imagine that you can ignite the spark in others, simply with a loving smile – watch as this wonderful feeling begins to spread.

'Music is well said to be the speech of angels.'

THOMAS CARLYLE

In the corner of the bedroom an angel was standing. It was not a dream and neither was it the first time an angel had woken this man from his sleep. He was being shown another vision. As he watched, he saw clearly an ancient battle and the bloodshed. In the next sequence he saw many soldiers of the First World War, marching along singing 'It's a long way to Tipperary, it's a long way from home'. He knew intuitively that the 'home' they sang about was Heaven.

Then came the third sequence with an eerie silence. He saw beautiful countryside, trees and grass, but the sky and the air around were copper-coloured; there was no birdsong or any sign of life. He knew this was a sign of the future. A world with no sign of life.

Then from the sky millions of pieces of paper started raining down and in an instant he knew what they were, he could read them all. They were pages from the Gospels giving the parables in the words of Jesus.

At that moment, in the most glorious tenor voice as clear and as beautiful as you would expect an angel to have, the angel sang the

words of an old song. This time the meaning hit like a bolt through the heart. 'Ah sweet mystery of life at last I've found thee ... 'tis love and love alone the world is seeking.' The message of the angel was loud and clear. We must all return to love and love one another, before it is too late.

Joyful laughter is music to the ears of angels.

When children laugh together at something it really is infectious. We know the benefits of serotonin produced in the brain by a really good laugh. Our lives are truly meant to be joyful. Joy is the expression of our true unbound nature, when our hearts and minds are free from impediments.

Joy is expressed in laughter and sometimes in tears of gratitude. It is felt when we are in harmony with others, ourselves and the beauty surrounding us. If one of the angels' tasks is to increase joy in our lives then our laughter must surely be like music to their ears.

If you are troubled by disharmony, or feel a lack of joy, put on some favourite music, close your eyes for a moment and invite Archangel Jophiel and the Angels of Joy to surround you. Imagine the angels smiling and dancing around you. Visualize joining them and laughing. Now bring that feeling slowly back with you into this moment. The more you do that makes your heart sing, the more often you are creating joy in your life.

Angels always have a hidden agenda – love.

The Angels of Light work according to God's plan alone, not as our servants but as our guides and protectors. They come to us for no other reason than to help us know and experience Divine love for ourselves. Ask the Archangel Raphael to help you tap into this love.

Archangel Raphael,
place your healing hands on my heart. I fully release any pain that I am holding there into your light. I trust that, as you dissolve the scars with your love and healing energy, you will enable me to give and receive true unconditional love.
Thank you.

Your angels are not there to judge you, only to love you.

You are the harshest judge of your own behaviour. Once you make a decision to work at areas in your life that may need some adjustment, ask the angels to help you soften your negative self-judgement with love.

Ask Archangel Zadkiel to help you to dissolve painful memories, to let go of judgement of self and others, and to enhance the spiritual gifts of forgiveness, tolerance and mercy. Visualize yourself surrounded by a warm healing violet light that cleanses and purifies negative traits and painful memories that affect your dealings with others. Allow yourself to bathe in this wonderful energy and feel refreshed and renewed.

'Children believe in angels and the feelings are mutual.'

KAREN GOLDMAN

Ben, aged four, had been very sad since his Daddy had gone away. He hadn't eaten well, couldn't sleep and even refused to play with his toys. His lovely mother Sue was beside herself with worry for her son and herself, but had read about the help of angels and came to see me to find out more.

In the week prior to her consultation, Ben came down from his room one evening after he had been put to bed and said: 'Mummy, there is a shiny lady in my room all dressed in white who knows who I am. I don't know what she wants but she keeps smiling and talking to me. Mummy, she is SO beautiful.'

Following the visit of the 'beautiful white lady', Ben became his normal happy self again, playing, eating and sleeping like a healthy little boy. Could it be that we need to return to innocence in order to actually see the angels for ourselves?

Angels bring light to the darkest moments.

Elly was very depressed. Her parents had split up and the family seemed to be falling apart, leaving her afraid and insecure. She was fifteen.

One night she woke from a fretful sleep to a feeling of heavy darkness approaching her with a suffocating sense of approaching doom. Instantly and instinctively she prayed for help and a white light appeared in her room. 'Are you sure this is what you want, Eleanor?' said a gentle female voice. 'Let me show you something.'

Elly saw a vision of her father sitting at his desk with his head in his hands, weeping. She then saw her mother sitting on a bed looking through old photographs, and she was also silently sobbing. Next she saw a vision of her older brother in his room, also looking through old photos, and this time she could see that they were pictures of them both as children. She realized that they were all grieving her death.

Tears poured down her cheeks as she felt their pain. 'Please help me,' she said. 'I don't want this to happen.' 'Then I'll protect you,' said the voice. Elly saw the light expand through her room and the darkness fade away like a moving shadow.

At the foot and sides of her bed she saw the shapes of three tall men with what she described as golden light around them which stretched between them, and, although she didn't dare to look, she knew there was a fourth angel behind her. She knew that she need never be afraid of the dark again.

An angel's greatest gift is presence in the present.

Isn't it strange how we are often unhappy no matter what we already have? Materially, we desire the lifestyles of others, their wealth or possessions, which we think will make our lives better. We are always craving. Buddha taught that this attachment to wanting is what creates human suffering. Remember that the past has already gone and is now history. The future is unknown and remains a mystery. That is why the gift is in the present. Try the following to let go and be in the moment.

Sit quietly and draw your attention to nothing but your breathing. As you breathe in deeply and then exhale, feel the air on the inside of your nostrils. Don't think of anything else but the air and your slow breathing in and out. Do this for five minutes at first, gradually increasing to fifteen minutes. By practising regularly you will develop the Zen technique of being 'in the now'. Enjoy your present!

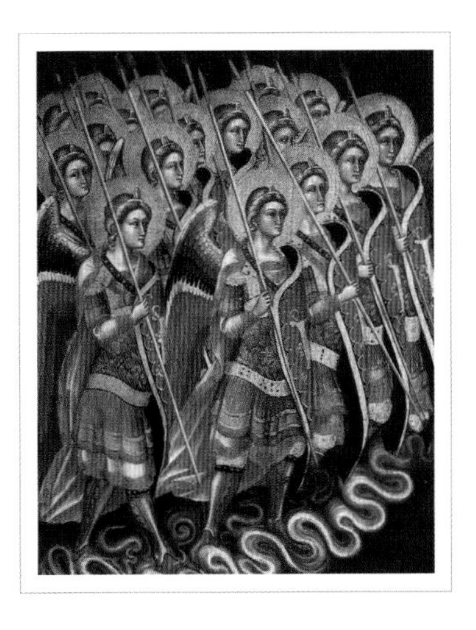

Angelic Connections

Our deeds fashion our destiny. Heaven and Hell are in our own hands.

Heaven is the divine connection to unconditional love and Hell is our fear of separation from it. When we think, act and live with love, all is harmonious. When we think, act and live in fear, then everything is surrounded by disharmony and difficulty.

Sit for a moment and breathe deeply. Imagine that you are inhaling a wonderful pink mist that is swirling all around you. As you inhale, breath the pink mist into your entire body, and as you exhale let go of all your worries and tensions. Affirm that you are totally supported by the Universe. Call to Archangel Michael, thank him for his protection and ask that all fear be removed from your thoughts, that you may live in complete harmony with all aspects of life.

Your angels don't see your physical actions and deeds, only the intentions in your mind.

Angels are working in accordance with Divine law. Their only interest is to assist humanity to evolve into the light. In Buddhism there is a belief that each of us has a 'Buddha-nature' that is capable of attaining Nirvana, or enlightenment, for ourselves.

One of the methods of finding our pathway to the light is that of 'right intention'; the idea is that it is not so much the action you take but the thought behind it. In your heart you are aware of your actions, and that you must hold the intention to do no harm. Some who have reached enlightenment have developed such immeasurable compassion that they choose to remain as Bodhisattvas to help us on that path. This is like the work of the archangels and great Ascended Masters who strive with us on many levels, lovingly guiding our route to union with the Divine, if that is our choice.

Angels know you are user-friendly, they simply follow the maker's instructions printed in your heart.

I spent many years struggling with a feeling that there was something I was meant to be doing. Not with each moment, but with my entire life. Being a mother was a wonderful experience for me, but it wasn't it. Returning to a nursing career was rewarding and fulfilling, but still wasn't it. I began searching everywhere for answers. I saw psychics, mediums, palmists and astrologers, and even had my aura repaired, but still couldn't establish my true purpose in life.

Then I decided to pray ardently, offering myself in service knowing that, when I really meant it and was ready, the signs would appear. I finally saw a course in 'healing with the angels' and signed up for it. My guide told me: 'Welcome Christine, we've been expecting you. Your work will be arduous but we are here to support and guide you.'

Each of us has a soul purpose, a destiny to fulfil. The angels know it, they see the plan in our DNA and they are waiting for us to decide to go ahead.

An angel may reach for your hand and touch your heart.

There is a saying that 'once you hit the bottom the only way left is up'. Many of us have felt the absolute emptiness of despair. Whether caused by depression, bankruptcy, isolation, abandonment, abuse (self or other), alcohol or drugs, despair is like falling into a deep hole. It is at this point many of us turn to God.

When the soul cries out for help it is never denied. Angels respond immediately to your call. They will take your hand if you wish and pull you from the pit. This may happen physically, emotionally or mentally. The overwhelming sense of love, wellbeing and gratitude this creates in your heart can hardly be described. Even better is the fact that, once you have experienced it, the memory will never leave you.

If you want to know where Heaven is, stop looking at your feet!

Have you ever noticed how many of us shuffle along with our shoulders hunched over as if we carried the weight of the world on our backs? With our eyes focused on the ground in front of us, we miss much of the beauty around us. In the angelic hierarchy, nature Devas and spirits are as important as the rest. We connect with these beings by practising awareness of the beauties in nature.

Look up. Don't miss the butterfly flirting with the breeze, or the sparkling dew on the spider's web. Watch the speed and grace of the clouds racing across the sky. When you see the wonders of nature, send these angels thoughts of gratitude and appreciation for the manifold beauties of this Heavenly world.

The next time you lean against a tree, ask a question from your heart. The answer will come from that sense of calm you get from the essence of the tree – from the angel that is its vital spirit.

When you look at life through the eyes of an angel, everything is in glowing colour.

Have you ever really looked at the leaves on a tree as they turn in the breeze and noticed the intricacy of their form? Have you noticed that the flowers adorning the chestnut are like tiny orchids when you examine them individually? Have you stood recently and watched the sunset? When you consider every particle of God's creation in its fine detail, and really see the beauty in everything, you are seeing life as it is truly meant to be seen.

When you begin to see through the eyes of an angel you cease judging others from a human perspective. Every situation, every encounter, everyone you meet has an inner beauty. Life takes on a brighter hue that is always visible through the loving angelic eyes.

Many hearts make 'light' work.

This is a twist on the old proverb 'many hands make light work'. The same principle applies here, but with a more spiritual message. Light refers to the all-encompassing universal Divine love which we imagine as a great light, often seen by mystics as a beautiful, awesome and intense light too bright to look upon.

Light also means wisdom. When one refers to working in the light, it means the light of God's wisdom that shines with true Divine love that brings healing and peace into the darkness. When many like-minded hearts are filled with this love, the 'light' begins to work.

THE GREAT INVOCATION

From the point of Light within the Mind of God
Let light stream forth into the minds of men.
Let light descend on Earth.
From the point of Love within the Heart of God
Let love stream forth into the hearts of men.
May Christ return to Earth.
From the centre where the Will of God is known
Let purpose guide the little wills of men –
The purpose which the Masters know and serve.
From the centre which we call the race of men
Let the Plan of Love and Light work out
And may it seal the door where evil dwells.
Let Light and Love and Power restore the Plan on Earth.

The air supporting the wings of an angel is the breath of a whisper of God's love.

At the centre of all creation is love – in the rain, the earth, the petal of a flower, the fur of a kitten, the wing of a bee. Love is in the sleeping face of a child, the song of a blackbird, the twinkling of a star. Love is in the roar of the ocean as it crashes on to the shore, the delicate intricacy of a snowflake, the lightness of a feather.

Love is in the whisper, the whistle, the rustle, the rush, the strength and the power of the wind. The same wind that fuels a tornado also gently caresses your face in the breeze. The wind that carries messages of fortune or disaster is the same wind that gives support beneath the wings of an angel. Your wings too.

An angel's kindness is an act of worship.

There are said to be nine choirs of angels. Archangels represent the different aspects of the nature of God while at the same time adoring their Creator. At the top of the hierarchy are the Seraphim who spend all their time singing in glory to God. Divine loving energy cascades through the tiers of angels down to those who are closer to us.

Those angels at the lower end of the hierarchy are also working through, with and in honour of Divine love. Everything they do for us is an act of worship. As this continuing, circulating angelic energy that passes down to us is worship, so too is every kindness that we perform on impulse without expecting a reward, given unconditionally and truly from the heart.

'He shall give his angels charge over thee,
to keep thee in all thy ways.'

PSALM 91:11

ANGEL PRAYER

*In the name of 'I am that I am' I detach and
let go of all energy in truth that is not mine.
I call back to myself all energy in truth that is mine and ask
that as it comes back to me,
it may be dissolved in the love and the light.*

*I call to the seven archangels and their legions of light,
I call to beloved Archangel Zadkiel and the Angels of Joy.
To Archangel Gabriel and the Angels of Wisdom,
to Archangel Michael and the Angels of Protection,
to Archangel Jophiel and the Angels of Illumination,
to Archangel Raphael and the Angels of Healing,
to Archangel Uriel and the Angels of Peace
and to Archangel Chamuel and the Angels of Love.*

With gratitude in my heart I ask you to enter my Earthly affairs and bring to me your wonderful Heavenly qualities.
Give me please the freedom from fear and self-doubt,
fill my mind with your wisdom,
illumination, understanding, inspiration, creativity,
knowledge and clearness of sight.

Help me to fully appreciate and enjoy the qualities of giving and receiving unconditional love, to feel compassion, mercy and forgiveness.
Show me how to dissolve the feelings of selfishness, self-condemnation and low self-esteem.
Give me the guidance I need to create inner peace and tranquillity in my heart and mind and a truly spiritual balance in my humanness.
I ask that with the love and guidance of God, the source of all life and love, and the help of the angels I will grow to reach the understanding of true Christ consciousness.
As I ask, with honest intent, so it may be so. Amen.

'If you see the angel in everyone you meet, you will always be in Divine company.'

KAREN GOLDMAN

If our souls are everlasting, through many lifetimes, and if we wait in a heavenly place until our rebirth, then we spend most of that time among the angelic realms. Following this thought, perhaps what we see in meditation is a memory. A part of us knows that angelic presence,and a spark of it remains in our hearts for all time.

When we are born, part of our soul – the ego-less, non-physical part – remains in the Heavenly place of love's existence. The higher self is wiser and purer than our bodily form, our corporeal self, and has no material attachment. It is possible to connect and ask our higher self for guidance in our lives. When we tap into the wisdom of our higher self we can also connect with the angel within us.

Next time you meet, notice the difference in the energy of your interaction when you allow the angel within you to connect with another at a deep soul level.

Beyond the visible softness of an angel is a force of purity that the world can never break.

This force is in the very softness of the dawn sky. It can be sensed in the distant twinkle of stars. It can be felt underfoot on a mossy river-bank, in the soft yielding of a white sandy beach. It can be stroked in the softness of a child's hair. It is in the intricate feather left behind as a message from the angels. It is in the filtered sunlight through the canopy of trees. It is in the promise of the rainbow. Yet its strength supports with the salty buoyancy of the ocean and the unbreakable pull of magnetic polarity. It supports the hardness of rock, the very substance of our planet, refined through time. Seemingly fragile yet containing the unbreakable and everlasting promise that is contained in angelic protection and love.

Daily invocations of the Essenes

Daily communion with the angels brings their guiding energies into our lives. One of the most powerful methods is to use the Essene communions which have been practised for over two millennia. The Essenes believe that seven angels of the Heavenly Father oversee the night, and seven angels of the Earthly Mother oversee the day. The daily invocations are as follows.

Saturday morning: The Earthly Mother and I are one, she gives the food of life to my whole body. **Saturday evening:** Angel of Eternal Life, descend upon me and give eternal life to my spirit.

Sunday morning: Angel of Earth, enter my physical being and regenerate my whole body. **Sunday evening:** Angel of Creative Work, descend upon humanity and give abundance to all mankind.

Monday morning: Angel of Life, enter my limbs and give strength to my whole body. **Monday evening:** Peace, peace, peace, Angel of Peace, be always everywhere.

Tuesday morning: Angel of Joy, descend upon Earth and give beauty to all beings. **Tuesday evening:** Angel of Power, descend upon my acting body and direct all my acts.

Wednesday morning: Angel of Sun, enter my solar centre and give the fire of life to my whole body. **Wednesday evening:** Angel of Love, descend upon my feeling body and purify all my feelings.

Thursday morning: Angel of Water, enter my blood and give the water of life to my whole body. **Thursday evening:** Angel of Wisdom, descend upon my thinking body and enlighten all my thoughts.

Friday morning: Angel of Air, enter my lungs and give the air of life to my whole body. **Friday evening:** The Heavenly Father and I are one.

INDEX

ACKNOWLEDGEMENTS

AUTHOR ACKNOWLEDGEMENTS
I would like to thank the Lucis Press for granting permission to reproduce The Great Invocation. I would also like to thank the following authors for their inspiration in the writing of this book:

Church, Anthea. *Angels*, Brahma Kumaris London, 1997

Cushnir, Howard Raphael. *Unconditional Bliss*, The Theosophical Publishing House, Wheaton Ill, 2000

Fox, Leonard and Rose, Donald L. (Eds). *Conversations with Angels*, Chrysalis Books, West Chester, PA., 1996

Goldman, Karen. *The Angel Book*, Simon & Schuster, New York, 1992

Heathcote-James, Emma. *Seeing Angels*, John Blake Publishing, London, 2001

Lambillion, Paul. *Being Loving is Being Healthy*, Fowler & Company, Romford, Essex, 1987

MacEwen, Anne. *Stepping Stones to a New Understanding*, Englang Publishing, Cirencester, 1991

Maclean, Dorothy. *To Honour the Earth*, HarperCollins, San Francisco, 1991

Szekeley, Edmond Bordeaux. *The Gospel of the Essenes*, C.W.Daniel Co.Ltd, Saffron Walden, Essex, 1974, 1993

Williamson, Marianne. *A Return to Love*, Thorsons, London, 1992,1996,

and many more ...

PICTURE ACKNOWLEDGEMENTS
AKG, London 1 centre, 91 bottom left; /Orsi Battaglini 14 top; /City Museum and Art Gallery, Birmingham 53 top; /Stefan Diller 39 top; /Pirozzi 44 top, 83 top; /Rabatti-Domingie 25 top, 63 right, 69 main, 75 top. **Bridgeman Art Library**, London/New York /The Barber Institute of Fine Arts, University of Birmingham 57 centre, 84 top; /Bristol City Museum and Art Gallery 60 top; /Bequest of Eleanor Clay Ford 2 main; /Galleria degli Uffizi, Florence 26 main, 43 centre; Lauros/ Giraudon 65 top; /Louvre, Paris 22 bottom left; /Museo Bottacin e Museo Civico, Padua 33 right; /National Gallery, London 9 main, 71 top; /Palazzo Medici Riccardi, Florence 6 top, 21 main; /Roy Miles Fine Paintings 51 top; /Sudley House, Liverpool 35 bottom right; /Vatican Museums and Galleries 10 main. **Corbis UK Ltd** /Albright-Knox Art Gallery 72 left; /Arte & Immaginisrl 54 top; /Elio Ciol 87 top; /Alinari Archives/Serge Domingie 40 left; /Francis G. Mayer 13 top, 18 bottom right, 78 bottom left, 81 top; /National Gallery Collection, London 17 bottom left, 47 right. **The Picture Desk Ltd.** /The Art Archive/Galleria Sabauda Turin/Dagli Orti 30 top; /Galleria Sabuda/Dagli Orti 5 main; Monte Maria Abbey, Burgusio Bolzano/Dagli Orti 29 bottom left, 66 bottom left; / Museo Civico Padua/Dagli Orti 77 main; /Palazzo dell' Arcivescovado Udine/Dagli Orti 59 centre; /Musee du Louvre, Paris/Dagli Orti 36 top.

Executive Editor Brenda Rosen
Managing Editor Clare Churly
Executive Art Editor Sally Bond
Designer Pia Ingham for Cobalt id
Picture Researchers Vickie Walters and Christine Junemann
Production Controller Aileen O'Reilly